D0865784

Please renew or return items by the date shown on your receipt

www.hertsdirect.org/libraries

Renewals and enquiries: 0300 123 4049

Textphone for hearing or speech impaired 0300 123 4041

Hertfordshire

Perfectly
POPPY

Beach Day Blues

Written by Michele Jakubowski

Illustrated by Erica-Jane Waters

Raintree is an imprint of Capstone Global Library Limited, a company incorporated in England and Wales having its registered office at 7 Pilgrim Street, London, EC4V 6LB – Registered company number: 6695582

www.raintreepublishers.co.uk
myorders@raintreepublishers.co.uk

Designers: Heather Kindseth Wutschke, Kristi Carlson and Philippa Jenkins
Editor: Catherine Veitch
Originated by Capstone Global Library Ltd
Printed and bound in China

ISBN 978 1 406 28047 0 (paperback)
18 17 16 15 14
10 9 8 7 6 5 4 3 2 1

British Library Cataloguing in Publication Data
A full catalogue record for this book is available from the British Library.

Contents

Chapter 1
Time to unload

"We're here!" Poppy cried as she jumped out of the car.

After a long drive with Poppy's family, Poppy and Millie were finally at the beach.

"Let's go!" Poppy shouted as she ran towards the sea.

"Not so fast," her mum called.

"You need to help carry things."

Poppy and Millie each grabbed a

beach bag. The bags were heavy, and

walking in the sand was tricky.

They helped set up the beach

umbrella, chairs and towels.

"Finished," Poppy said. "Now it's

time to swim!"

"Not so fast," said her mum again.

"What now?" Poppy asked. She was starting to think she'd never get to swim!

"You need sun cream," her mum said, holding up the bottle.

Poppy stood still while her mum

put sun cream on her. It took forever!

Finally her mum had finished.

Poppy asked, "Now can I swim?"

Her mum smiled and said, "Yes.

I'll come too."

Chapter 2

Beach blues

"Hooray!" Poppy and Millie

yelled as they raced down the beach.

They had been waiting weeks to go

swimming, and it was time to have

some fun!

Poppy and Millie ran into the
water. Poppy's mum watched.

"It's freezing!" Millie said as she
quickly ran back out of the water.

"But we have to swim!" Poppy said as she stood in the cold water.

She tried to splash around, but it wasn't fun to splash alone. Soon she began shivering. Then a big wave knocked her over.

This made Poppy grumpy. She

joined Millie on the beach.

"If we can't swim, what are we

supposed to do?" Poppy asked.

"We could play with the beach ball," Millie said.

Poppy and Millie tried throwing the ball back and forth. The wind made it hard to catch.

Poppy chased after the ball.

She tripped in the sand and fell

on her face.

"Ugh!" Poppy shouted. The sand

was sticking to her. It was really itchy.

"I'm going to rinse off the sand,"

Poppy told her mum, as she headed

for the showers.

She walked into the shower block.

Poppy wrinkled her nose. "Yuck!"

The floors were wet and sandy, and the room smelled fishy. In the corner was a shower.

Poppy turned on the shower. The water was freezing! She rinsed off the sand and grabbed her towel. Then she slipped and fell on the dirty floor.

Chapter 3

Sun and smiles

Poppy wanted to have the perfect beach day, but instead she had the beach day blues.

She was tired, dirty and hungry. She picked herself up and went to find her mum.

Then she began crying. "I don't like the beach!"

"Oh, Poppy," her mum said as she gave her a big hug.

Poppy's mum spread her towel under the umbrella. She gave Poppy a bottle of water and some crunchy apple slices.

Then Millie came running over. "What's wrong, Poppy?" she asked.

"I want to go home," Poppy said.

"But you were so excited about

coming to the beach," her mum said.

"I know I was. But the sea is too cold, and the wind is too windy," Poppy said.

"How about you play in the sand?" her mum asked.

"I tried that," Poppy said. "I fell on my face!"

"Let's build a sandcastle!" Millie said. "You won't fall down doing that. It will be fun."

"I guess," Poppy said, but she wasn't so sure.

Poppy and Millie began building
their sandcastle. At first it was small.
They made it bigger and bigger and
bigger. Then they collected seashells
to decorate it. It looked great!

"This is hard work! I'm getting hot," Poppy said.

"Me too," said Millie. "Should we try the water again?"

"I guess we could," said Poppy.

They walked slowly into the water with Poppy's mum close by. It still felt cold, but this time the cold felt good. They began splashing and jumping around.

"Good news!" Poppy said. "My beach day blues has become beach fun. I like the beach again!"

"What a relief!" Millie laughed as she splashed Poppy.

"You're telling me," replied Poppy with a huge smile.

Poppy's new words

I learned so many new words today! I wrote them down so that I could use them again.

collect gather things together

decorate add things to something to make it look prettier

relief feeling of freedom from pain or worry

rinse wash something in clean water

shiver shake with cold

suppose believe something is possible

wrinkle crease or line in something

Poppy's thoughts

After my day at the beach, I had some time to think. Here are some of my questions and thoughts from the day.

1. I was excited to go to the beach, but then so many things went wrong. I was really disappointed. Talk about a time when you were disappointed.

2. If you were me, would you have stayed at the beach or gone home early? Why?

3. Write a paragraph about your favourite things to do at the beach.

4. I didn't have the perfect beach day, but my mum said I was good to keep trying when things were difficult. She said I persevered. Talk about a time when you persevered.

Frozen grapes

When it's hot outside, nothing tastes better than some cold treats. Here is how I make frozen grapes, which are my favourite. My mum says they are a lot healthier than ice cream and taste just as good.

What you do:

1. Rinse the grapes.

2. Dry them off.

3. Wrap the grapes in a clean tea towel.

4. Put them in the freezer for a couple of hours.

5. Take out and enjoy. Easy and delicious!

Ask an adult for help

Beach day activities

Don't just lie around at the beach. Grab a friend and have some fun. Here are some of my favourite beach activities. Put on some sun cream and try them out!

- build a sandcastle

- jump over waves

- collect seashells

- bury your feet in the sand

- swim, swim, swim

- play catch with a beach ball

About the author

Michele Jakubowski grew up in Chicago, United States of America (USA). She has the teachers in her life to thank for her love of reading and writing. While writing has always been a passion for Michele, she believes it is the books she has read over the years, and the teachers who introduced them, that have made her the storyteller she is today. Michele lives in Ohio, USA, with her husband, John, and their children, Jack and Mia.

About the illustrator

Erica-Jane Waters grew up in the beautiful Northern Irish countryside, where her imagination was ignited by the local folklore and fairy tales. She now lives in Oxfordshire with her young family. Erica writes and illustrates children's books and creates art for magazines, greeting cards and various other projects.